W9-CKD-645

The Gift of Love

Compiled by **Evelyn Loeb**

Design by
Scharr Design

PETER PAUPER PRESS, INC.
WHITE PLAINS · NEW YORK

To my love, Nick

Copyright © 1991
Peter Pauper Press, Inc.
202 Mamaroneck Avenue
White Plains, New York 10601
ISBN 0-88088-217-4
Printed in Hong Kong
5   4   3

Table of Contents

For love is heaven,

and heaven is love.

SIR WALTER SCOTT

Sonnet

Shall I compare thee to a Summer's day?
Thou art more lovely and more temperate:
Rough winds do shake the darling buds of
    May,
And Summer's lease hath all too short a date:
Sometime too hot the eye of heaven shines,
And often is his gold complexion dimmed;
And every fair from fair sometime declines,
By chance or nature's changing course
    untrimmed:
But thy eternal Summer shall not fade
Nor lose possession of that fair thou owest;
Nor shall Death brag thou wanderest in his
    shade,
When in eternal lines to time thou growest:
So long as men can breathe, or eyes can see,
So long lives this, and this gives life to thee.

WILLIAM SHAKESPEARE

Love Letter
from Napoleon to Josephine

I don't love you, not at all; on the contrary, I detest you—You're a naughty, gawky, foolish Cinderella. You never write me; you don't love your husband; you know what pleasure your letters give him, and yet you haven't written him six lines, dashed off casually!

What do you do all day, Madam? What is the affair so important as to leave you no time to write to your devoted lover? What affection stifles and puts to one side the love, the tender and constant love you promised him? Of what sort can be that marvelous being, that new lover who absorbs every moment, tyrannizes over your days, and prevents your giving any attention to your husband? Josephine, take care! Some fine night, the doors will be broken open, and there I'll be.

Indeed, I am very uneasy, my love, at receiving no news of you; write me quickly four pages, pages full of agreeable things which shall fill my heart with the pleasantest feelings.

I hope before long to crush you in my arms and cover you with a million kisses burning as though beneath the equator.

BONAPARTE

When, in 1839, Benjamin Disraeli married the widow Mary Anne Wyndham Lewis, a woman 12 years older than he, he married her fortune and London townhouse as well. The marriage turned out to be a happy one, however—though Disraeli often teased his wife that he had wed her only for her money. "But," she would always answer, "if you had to do it again, you'd do it for love!"

Know you the land where the lemon-trees bloom? In the dark foliage the gold oranges glow, a soft wind hovers from the sky, the myrtle is still and the laurel stands tall—do you know it well? There, there, I would go, O my beloved, with thee!

JOHANN WOLFGANG VON GOETHE

Flower and Herb Symbolism

Special occasions, such as weddings, Valentine's Day, anniversaries, and births, call for symbolic potpourri ingredients. One feels a strong attraction to certain plants, perhaps because of something felt, in addition to their beauty and fragrance. Renaissance painters evoked the emotions of love and hate by portraying bouquets of flowers. Herbs and their symbolic meanings have become one with the giving of flowers. The following recipe should delight the grower, maker, or receiver of potpourri, and give increased insight into the realm of plants.

Potpourri D'Amour

Plant:	**Symbolic Meaning:**
1 cup heliotrope	*Devotion*
1 cup myrtle	*Love*
½ cup pansy	*Thoughts*
½ cup peach blossom	*I am your captive*
½ cup red clover	*Industry*
1 cup rudbeckia	*Justice*
1 cup sage	*Wisdom, virtue*
½ cup xeranthemum	*Cheerfulness under adversity*

I love you for ignoring the possibilities of the fool and weakling in me, and for laying firm hold on the possibilities of the good in me.

I love you for closing your ears to the discords in me, and for adding to the music in me by worshipful listening.

I love you because you are helping me to make of the timber of my life not a tavern, but a temple, and of the words of my every day not a reproach, but a song.

I love you because you have done more than any creed could have done to make me happy.

You have done it without a touch, without a word, without a sign.

You have done it first by being yourself.

After all, perhaps this is what love means.

ANONYMOUS

Strawberry Shortcake

5	cups strawberries
5	tablespoons sugar
2	cups unbleached flour
2	tablespoons baking powder
1/4	teaspoon salt
1/3	cup unsalted butter
3/4	cup cold milk
2	cups heavy cream

Wash, hull, and halve strawberries, and place them in a bowl. Sprinkle 3 tablespoons of sugar over berries.

Preheat oven to 450°. Sift flour, baking powder, and salt together. Cut butter into dry ingredients until it resembles coarse meal. Make a well and add milk quickly, forming dough into a ball. Roll dough out on a floured surface to 1/2-inch thickness. Cut dough with a biscuit cutter or glass. Bake in a 400° oven for 10-12 minutes.

Pour heavy cream into a bowl. Add 2 tablespoons of sugar and whip. Cut biscuits in half. Place a halved biscuit in a serving plate. Add some strawberries. Cover with top half of biscuit. Add more strawberries and whip cream. Serves 8.

Annabel Lee

It was many and many a year ago,
In a kingdom by the sea
That a maiden there lived whom you may
   know
By the name of Annabel Lee;—
And this maiden she lived with no other
   thought
Than to love and be loved by me.

I was a child and *she* was a child,
In this kingdom by the sea,
But we loved with a love that was more than
   love—
I and my Annabel Lee—
With a love that the wingèd seraphs of
   Heaven
Coveted her and me.

And this was the reason that, long ago,
In this kingdom by the sea,
A wind blew out of a cloud, chilling
My beautiful Annabel Lee;
So that her high-born kinsmen came
And bore her away from me,
To shut her up in a sepulcher
In this kingdom by the sea.

The angels, not half so happy in Heaven,
Went envying her and me,—
Yes!—that was the reason (as all men know,
In this kingdom by the sea)
That the wind came out of the cloud by night,
Chilling and killing my Annabel Lee.

But our love it was stronger by far than the
    love
Of those who were older than we—
Of many far wiser than we—
And neither the angels in Heaven above,
Nor the demons down under the sea,
Can ever dissever my soul from the soul
Of the beautiful Annabel Lee:—

For the moon never beams without bringing
    me dreams
Of the beautiful Annabel Lee;
And the stars never rise but I feel the bright
    eyes
Of the beautiful Annabel Lee;
And so, all the night-tide, I lie down by the
    side
Of my darling,—my darling,—my life and my
    bride,
In the sepulcher there by the sea—
In her tomb by the sounding sea.

EDGAR ALLAN POE

To My Dear and Loving Husband

If ever two were one, then surely we.
If ever man were lov'd by wife, then thee.
If ever wife was happy in a man,
Compare with me, ye women, if you can.
I prize thy love more than whole Mines of
   gold,
Or all the riches that the East doth hold.
My love is such that Rivers cannot quench,
Nor ought but love from thee give
   recompence.
Thy love is such I can no way repay;
The heavens reward thee manifold I pray.
Then while we live, in love lets so persever,
That when we live no more, we may live
   ever.

ANNE BRADSTREET.

A Lovers' Menu
Dinner for Two in Red

Appetizer:
   Angel Hair Pasta with Tomato Sauce

Salad:
   Radicchio and Endive

Entree:
   Filet Mignon
   Baked Tomatoes
   Redskin Potatoes

   Bordeaux

Dessert
   Strawberry Shortcake
   Pink Champagne

Set a beautiful table using your best china and sparkling silver. Add a fragrant bouquet of pink roses. Turn down the lights and light the candles. Play your favorite love songs. Enjoy a wonderful dinner for two and romance will flourish.

You bound strong sandals on my feet,
   You gave me bread and wine,
And sent me under sun and stars,
   For all the world was mine.

Oh take the sandals off my feet,
   You know not what to do;
For all my world is in your arms,
   My sun and stars are you.

SARA TEASDALE

I think true love is never blind,
   But rather brings an added light,
An inner vision quick to find
   The beauties hid from common sight.

No soul can ever clearly see
   Another's highest, noblest part,
Save through the sweet philosophy
   And loving wisdom of the heart.

PHOEBE CARY

If thou must love me, let it be for naught
Except for love's sake only. Do not say:
"I love her for her smile, . . . her look, . . .
   her way
Of speaking gently, . . . for a trick of thought
That falls in well with mine, and certes
   brought
A sense of pleasant ease on such a day";—
For these things in themselves, Beloved, may
Be changed, or change for thee,—and love so
   wrought
May be unwrought so. Neither love me for
Thine own dear pity's wiping my cheeks dry,
Since one might well forget to weep who bore
Thy comfort long, and lose thy love thereby.
But love me for love's sake, that evermore
Thou mayst love on through love's eternity.

ELIZABETH BARRETT BROWNING

Love Gods

The Romans knew her as VENUS, the goddess of love, beauty, and fertility. The Greeks called her APHRODITE, for they believed that she arose from the *aphros* or foam of the sea. Lovely beyond compare, Aphrodite drifted among the Greek Islands before at last reaching the home of the gods on Mount Olympus.

Aphrodite immediately entranced Zeus, but when she would not give herself to him, he forced her to marry his lame son Hephaestus, the blacksmith. The marriage was an unhappy one, and Aphrodite indulged in many love affairs. From her most famous liaison, with Ares the god of war, came five children, including EROS (or CUPID to the Romans) who came to symbolize love.

The most noteworthy of Aphrodite's other attachments was her love of Adonis, the mortal huntsman. Adonis, however, did not return the goddess' affection, but rather preferred the thrill of the hunt. In spite of Aphrodite's warnings to take care, Adonis was killed one day in the woods by a wild boar. His spirit instantly descended to the underworld and into the arms of its queen, Persephone. Heartbroken, Aphrodite appealed to Zeus to bring Adonis back, but by then Persephone also loved Adonis, and asked Zeus to leave the hunter with her.

Zeus, caught between two goddesses, declared in Solomonic fashion that Adonis would spend six months a year with each one. When Adonis resides in the underworld, the earth becomes chilly, then cold and barren, as in autumn and winter, but when he returns above to Aphrodite, her joy transforms the world into the bloom of spring and summer.

Eros, the son of Aphrodite, caused mortals and gods alike to fall irrevocably in love, simply by wounding them with one of his invisible arrows. He can claim credit for the loves of Medea and Jason, Dido's passion for Aeneas, and his own mother's adoration of Adonis. Eros is often depicted as blindfolded, perhaps to explain the often unlikely alliances he induces.

Indeed, even Eros was subject to his own random powers. He accidentally wounded himself with an arrow while on a mission for Aphrodite, and fell in love with the beautiful mortal girl Psyche. Ironically, Aphrodite had wanted Psyche to fall in love with a lowly mortal so that Psyche's beauty would no longer rival her own. Eros, ruled by his passion for Psyche, came to her every night, but in order to guard her from Aphrodite's jealous wrath, never allowed her to see his person in the light. One night, however, overcome by curiosity, Psyche lit a lamp in order to view at last the man she loved.

Astonished by Eros' beauty, Psyche inadvertently spilled a drop of hot oil on him, and awoke him from his slumber. Eros flew away instantly, in spite of his continued love for Psyche, and left her in despair. The lovers were eventually reconciled after Psyche performed three arduous tasks to appease Aphrodite, and Eros convinced Zeus to make Psyche immortal so that they could live together happily forever.

My life is a torn book. But at the end
A little page, quite fair, is saved, my friend,
Where thou didst write thy name.

EDWARD ROBERT BULWER-LYTTON

Heart-Shaped
Sugar Cookies

½   cup soft butter
½   cup sugar
1   egg
1   tablespoon milk or cream
½   teaspoon vanilla
½   teaspoon lemon extract
1½   cups flour
1   teaspoon cream of tartar
½   teaspoon baking soda
¼   teaspoon salt

Combine ingredients in above order. Chill dough. Roll out very thin, about ⅛ of an inch. Cut into heart shapes with cookie cutter, sprinkle with red-colored sugar, and bake at 350° on greased cookie sheets until very lightly browned—about 8-10 minutes. Watch carefully to keep from over-browning. One recipe makes about 80 small cookies.

Parting

My life closed twice before its close;
It yet remains to see
If Immortality unveil
A third event to me.

So huge, so hopeless to conceive
As these that twice befell.
Parting is all we know of heaven
And all we need of hell.

EMILY DICKINSON

Doubt that the stars are fire;
Doubt that the sun doth move;
Doubt truth to be a liar;
But never doubt I love.

WILLIAM SHAKESPEARE,
Hamlet

Ideal
Astrological Love Matches

Aries	⧉	Leo
Aries	⧉	Sagittarius
Taurus	⧉	Virgo
Taurus	⧉	Capricorn
Cancer	⧉	Scorpio
Cancer	⧉	Pisces
Leo	⧉	Sagittarius
Virgo	⧉	Capricorn
Libra	⧉	Gemini
Libra	⧉	Aquarius
Scorpio	⧉	Pisces
Aquarius	⧉	Gemini

Set Me As a Seal

Set me as a seal upon thine heart;
As a seal upon thine arm:
For love is strong as death;
Jealousy is cruel as the grave,
The flashes thereof are flashes of fire,
A very flame of the Lord.
Many waters cannot quench love,
Neither can the floods drown it. . . .

KING SOLOMON

Lovers' Potpourri

One of the most popular, endearing and traditional uses of potpourri is to strengthen feelings of love and family togetherness on holidays and at gatherings in the home. At these times, people come together to reflect, share, and rejoice. The use of home-made potpourri can enrich these occasions with visual, scent-filled, and tasty treats.

1   cup rose petals
1   cup rose hips
½   cup rosemary leaves
½   cup red dianthus blossoms
½   cup bachelor's button blossoms
       and leaves
1   cup honeysuckle flowers
½   cup mint leaves (apple mint best)

These herbs and flowers, dried in the summer and autumn, and stored in a closed, dark container, give a whiff of early spring and some lovable whimsy to Valentine's Day. Fragrance evokes what words may fail to express. Give a tin of potpourri filled with your heart's wishes to a friend or loved one. The day will linger, the feelings will have substance.

Herbal Love Bath

Ingredients:

1 cup lavender
1 cup rosemary
1 cup rose petals
½ cup rose geranium leaves
½ cup lemon verbena leaves
1 tablespoon each thyme, mint, sage,
   and orrisroot powder

Method:

*Combine all ingredients. Mix thoroughly and keep in
a tightly lidded container. To make a bath ball, pack
¼ cup in a muslin square and tie securely. Bring to a
boil in 1 cup of water and let stand for 10 minutes.
Add the bath ball to hot bath water and use it to scrub
yourself. Relax in the bath and let your thoughts focus
on romance.*

Believe Me If All Those Endearing Young Charms

Believe me, if all those endearing young
  charms
Which I gaze on so fondly today
Were to fade by tomorrow and fleet in
  my arms
Like fairy gifts fading away,
Thou wouldst still be adored as this
  moment thou art,
Let thy loveliness fade as it will,
And around the dear ruin each wish of
  my heart
Would entwine itself verdantly still.

It is not while beauty and youth are thine
  own
And thy cheeks unprofaned by a tear
That the fervor and faith of a soul can be
  known
To which time will but make thee more dear.
No, the heart that has truly loved never
  forgets
But as truly loves on to the close—
As the sunflower turns on her god when he
  sets
The same look which she turned when he
  rose.

THOMAS MOORE

What's the earth
  With all its art, verse, music, worth—
  Compared with love, found, gained, and kept?

ROBERT BROWNING

The essence of all beauty, I call love.
The attribute, the evidence, and end,
The consummation to the inward sense
Of beauty apprehended from without,
I still call love.

ELIZABETH BARRETT BROWNING

Filet in Wine Sauce

2   filet steaks (1 inch thick)
2   strips of bacon
2   tablespoons butter
    Salt and pepper
¼   cup beef stock
1   teaspoon tomato paste
⅛   cup of Madeira
1   tablespoon minced parsley

Wrap each steak with a strip of bacon. Secure bacon with toothpick. Melt butter in a heavy skillet. Brown the steaks. Sauté three to four minutes on each side. Immediately remove meat from heat. Discard the strings and bacon. Season filets with salt and pepper. Keep meat warm while preparing the sauce. Pour fat out of the skillet. Stir in stock and add tomato paste. Bring to a boil, rapidly scraping up cooking juices. Pour in wine, stir and let simmer one minute. Add herbs, pour sauce over meat and serve.

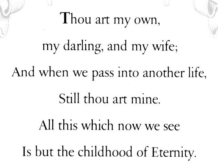

Thou art my own,

my darling, and my wife;

And when we pass into another life,

Still thou art mine.

All this which now we see

Is but the childhood of Eternity.

ARTHUR JOSEPH MUNBY